Dear Parents and Educators,

Welcome to *Bea is for Business*™, an innovative, educational platform dedicated to teaching young people about business. We believe strongly that business education needs to start early at school and at home. Our books are just the beginning. There's also a website, www.beaisforbusiness.com, where you and your child can explore a variety of business topics, vocabulary, classroom curriculums, focus groups, and do-at-home activities.

All the activities and opportunities included in the *Bea is for Business* educational platform are built off the Common Core State Standards and aim to do the following:

- help teach basic business principles and monetary concepts

- expand business vocabulary and language

- create learning opportunities for kids to think differently and solve problems creatively

- foster an environment of feedback and encouragement

- inspire kids to be entrepreneurs as they conceive or implement business ideas

Reading this book might inspire your child's own business ideas. Parents, that's where you come in. Please sit down with your child and talk through ideas. You are welcome to submit any business concepts to our website. Bea can then serve as a consultant for your child's business idea. We hope to hear from you. More importantly, we hope this begins a new learning journey that inspires the next generation of entrepreneurs.

All the best,

Jamie A. Brown & Meg Seitz

To HP and GT - for showing up the last 36 years - with a lot of love. J.B.

To Mom, Daddy, and Maret; #thankyou #loveyou. To the WFU MBA ladies; #businessgirlsruletheworlds. To S.H., with love. M.S.

To my family and my home support team: Neyda, Ariana & Giancarlo. Thank you all! A.V.

Bea is for Business: The Party-Planning Venture

Text: Copyright © 2014, Bea is for Business, LLC

Illustrations: Copyright © 2014, Bea is for Business, LLC

Published by:

Bea is for Business, LLC, P.O. Box 3009, Charlotte, NC 28230

For more information and educational resources, please visit: www.beaisforbusiness.com

ISBN 978-0-9893403-2-8 (pbk) - ISBN 978-0-9893403-3-5 (ebook)

First Edition 2014

The Party-Planning Venture

By Jamie A. Brown & Meg Seitz

Illustrated By Arody J. Victoria

To Kate...

[signature]

I'm working in Mom's office upstairs. (It's the Bea is for Business office now, too.)

I just cannot come up with any good business ideas today. Nothing. Nada. Nil. Zilch.

I snap back to reality. My friend, Makayla, will be here any minute to play.

The doorbell rings.

"Beatrice!" Dad shouts. "Makayla is here!
I'm sending her upstairs to your office."

Dad is one great assistant.

"Hey, Bea! Nice view," Makayla says as she peers out the window.

"Thank you!" I smile. "So, what's new?"

Makayla hands me a card. It's a party invitation.

"It inspired me," she says. "I want to start a business to plan and manage parties for kids."

"Cool! A party-planning business sure would help busy parents. You could create a fun theme, plan the party activities, and then be there to help," I say. "I think you're onto something!"

"Yes," Makayla confirms. "But, I don't know how to get my business started."

I take a deep breath. I'm not exactly sure either.

Mom helped me think through some important questions when I started Bea is for Business. Maybe those same questions will help Makayla:

1. What is the business's name?

2. How will you let people know about it?

3. How will your business be the most helpful to people?

4. How much will someone pay for your help?

"For now, let's just tackle Question #1. Do you have a name for your business?" I ask.

Makayla perks up. "I want to call it P.F.K.—Parties for Kids."

"Jackpot!" I shout. "That's a great name!"

"We can save the other questions for tomorrow," I say. "Let's play outside before it gets dark!"

The next afternoon, I'm hanging out at the very top of the neighborhood park's playhouse. I'm brainstorming. For Question #2, how can we let people know about Makayla's business?

A few ideas come to mind. I write them down.

"Bea!" Mom calls. "It's time to head home."

I poke my head down a tunnel. "Mom, may I please have five more minutes? I'm thinking of ideas for Makayla's business."

Mom smiles. "How's it going?" she asks.

"Well, I could use some help," I say.

Mom climbs up into the playhouse and listens to my plan. She likes my ideas. She offers suggestions, too.

"How about this," Mom says. "I know lots of moms who could use Makayla's help. I could email them. It would be a type of advertising for P.F.K."

"That's a great idea!" I say. "I think Question #2 is covered. Let's go home and write that email!"

Three days later, I have news. Seriously. B-I-G news.

I run to Makayla's. "We have a lead!" I shout. "Mrs. DeFault emailed. She wants your help planning Tommy DeFault's fourth birthday party!"

I reach into my bag. I pull out our original list of questions.

"We need to figure out Question #3," Makayla says.

"How about we come up with the perfect party theme?" I say.

"Yeah! That would be super helpful. And I know where we can get some ideas," Makayla says, holding up a magazine and her mom's tablet.

1. What is the business's name?

2. How will you let people know about it?

3. How will your business be the most helpful to people?

4. How much will someone pay for your help?

15

We start to research. We look through magazines and scroll through party-planning pictures on the tablet.

We notice a trend with a lot of the kids' parties...

SUPERHEROES!

"That's it! P.F.K. could help Mrs. DeFault plan a superhero party for Tommy," I say. "We'll have superhero games, a superhero cake, and superhero prizes."

"And a guest appearance by a superhero!" Makayla adds.

We look over the pictures and nod. We've got our answer to Question #3. Jackpot!

The next morning, I'm hustling to math. There's paint caked on my arm from art. I stop quickly at the water fountain to scrub it off.

I hear a long sigh from someone standing beside me. I turn around.

It's Nigel DeFault, Tommy's older brother. He's drumming his thumb on a tablet.

"My mom told me about you and Makayla," he says. "What makes you think *you* can plan a party?"

I look Nigel right in the eye. I'm trying to decide how to respond. Suddenly, Nigel interjects.

"You can count on me *not* being there," he says. "I'll be upstairs playing with my new tablet. It's the best one on the market. I call her 'Big Data.'"

I check my watch. I only have two minutes.

"I have to get to math, Nigel," I say. I hustle down
the hall.

In class, I try to keep my mind on Mr. Rich's lesson: multiplication.

All I can think about is P.F.K.—and Nigel. What if he's right? Maybe we *can't* plan a party.

'Be confident,' I say to myself. 'We can do this. We've made it through three quarters of the questions.'

All we need is an answer to Question #4: How much will parents pay us to help at a party?

"Bea?" Mr. Rich asks. "Bea, do you know the answer?"

I glance quickly up front.

"Yes," I say, refocusing. "Six times four is . . . 24."

"That's correct," Mr. Rich says.

'Wait! That's it!' I think. 'We will charge by the hour. That's how parents can pay us! We have a way to answer Question #4!'

I scribble more calculations into my notebook.

Makayla comes to my house after school.

"Mom, how much, per hour, would you pay us to plan a party?" I ask.

"About $12 an hour for both of you," she replies.

"Then on the day of the party," I say, "we'll do this calculation: # of hours (of work) x $12 = total."

With Mom's help, we email our estimate, the superhero party idea, and a supply list to Mrs. DeFault.

A couple hours later, Mrs. DeFault responds. She loves the idea. She's happy to pay us $12 an hour. And she'll buy all the supplies.

We're ready to party!

It's September 16th—the morning of the party. We arrive early to set up.

Soon, kids dressed as superheroes wander into the house.

"Let's start with 'Pin the Cape on the Superhero,'" Makayla says.

My best friend, Lander, is here with his sister, Maura. I paint their faces as they wait in line.

Suddenly, I see Nigel rush down the
steps clutching Big Data.

"What's going on?" he asks.

"We're celebrating superhero style," Mrs. DeFault
answers. "Thanks to these two smart girls!" She
points to Makayla and me.

"I didn't know you were doing ALL of this!" Nigel whispers to his mom. "Why didn't you message me?!"

"You said you were busy playing with your new tablet," Mrs. DeFault begins.

Nigel doesn't hear her. He has already set down Big Data to join the party.

"Time for cake!" yells Mr. DeFault, who bursts through the kitchen door dressed like a superhero.

Everyone goes wild!

The kids finish their cake and make their ways to the door. I hand out goodie bags.

"What a fun party," says Mrs. DeFault. "How much money do I owe you two for helping out today?"

I grab my notebook. I scribble down the calculation.

"That's $48, Mrs. DeFault. That will cover our four hours," I say. "Makayla and I are splitting the money."

"Sounds great," Mrs. DeFault answers.

It's pouring quarter-sized drops of rain outside, so we drive Makayla to her house.

Like always, I set aside a portion of my money to donate to my favorite animal shelter.

After we drop off Makayla, we take the long way home.

Our car stops at a traffic light. I see people scurrying through the rain to the neighborhood market.

I look closely. I see a man standing in the rain selling umbrellas. Then, it hits me.

"Mom!" I say. "Business ideas are absolutely *everywhere!*"

Mom smiles at me in the rearview mirror.

We pull into our driveway.

"Are you coming inside, Bea?" Mom asks.

"In a minute," I answer.

My notebook is out on my lap. I'm scribbling business ideas. In fact, I'm thinking of new ideas faster than I can write.

I will call them 'Big Ideas.' I cannot wait to tell Nigel that.

Made in the USA
Charleston, SC
11 October 2015